THE DAY MY SISTER GOT BAPTISED

THE SACRAMENTS SERIES | BAPTISM

Copyright © 2024 St Shenouda Press

All rights reserved. No part of this book may be reproduced in any manner without prior written permission from the publisher.

St Shenouda Press
8419 Putty Rd, Putty, NSW 2330
Sydney, Australia

www.stshenoudapress.com

ISBN 13: 978-1-7635450-7-6

Today's the day! Tommy leapt out of bed
so excited for the day ahead.
For today you see, is the day the priest
baptises his dear sister Bethany!

He runs out of his room and down the hall
and for his mum and dad he loudly calls.
He can't contain himself, he just can't wait
Oh how he needs to ensure they don't run late

They all get dressed and look their very best
Tommy even wears his new button-up vest
Bethany wears a dress with a

SPARKLING BOW

They all hop in the car
and off to church they go

At
✟ CHURCH ✟
the priest waits excitedly for them to arrive

In front of him the basin of water

where Bethany will soon take a dive

They pray prayers for safety
and protection from harm
and they each declare their love
for our Lord while raising their arms

Bethany is lovingly held by father and **DIPPED** three times into the water

All while

the deacons

SING

joyful praises

She then has the
Body and Blood of Christ
and the whole family celebrates
her being given new life

Around the church
they walk in a procession
Holding candles and praising
for this joyous occasion

What a day!
Oh, what a marvellous day!
They witnessed three different

SACRAMENTS

take place today
Baptism, Chrismation and
Holy Communion too
All working together
to make God's children new

You see, the baptism represents our new birth
While we receive the Holy Spirit during
Chrismation to guide us on this earth
Everyone sings and chants with joyful glee
For now, with God, we are one heavenly family

www.ingramcontent.com/pod-product-compliance
Lightning Source LLC
Chambersburg PA
CBHW041429190426
43193CB00049B/2983